This book is dedicated to those who helped me along the way, those who didn't and everyone in between.

If I were to choose a single soul to dedicate this book to, it would be Bijou the doodle for the rest of our days, but due to recent events, this book will forever be dedicated to the pug that went to soon.

Dr. Icarus Pug, Ph.D

09/09/17-09/30/21

Disclaimer:

This book contains content that refers to true events, all names used have been changed to ensure anonymity of persons described. Any real names used have been used with permission from the author to maintain dignity and confidentiality of all persons described.

Table of Contents

Pg. 4-52 The Origin Story of Brain Rollercoaster

P. 53-69 Finding Purpose in Unfamiliar

Pg. 70-81 The Chapter to Make Him Blush… the tale of the first five months of Wow & Computer Head

Pg. 82-95 Poetry Fun for Silly and Serious Times

Pg 96-100 A Finale Without a Drum Solo

Tightness in the chest, quickened breathing, tears: plentiful, this is how it always was. Anxiety at its full potential: picking me up and tossing me violently into a state in which I dreaded the most. The first fifteen and half years of my life were sprinkled with hundreds, if not thousands of these instances. But as quickly as those instances would occur, another event added itself to the mix. It was May 31st 2006. My mother had been on the phone that night and I couldn't sleep, not because I was anxious for the next set of my Provincial Achievement tests or because of something going on between my friends or peers at school, but because of voices outside. Unfortunately, those voices were unlike any voice I had ever heard before. They were the sounds of my brain quickly changing and for the worst. I was fifteen and psychotic.

    There's no way to put it lightly, my problems were only starting. I had no insight, just like anyone suffering from schizophrenia. To me, the voices, that happened to belong to two of my boyfriend at the time's friends, we very real. Just as quickly as it all happened I was in the Emergency room at the University of Alberta hospital in the wee hours of the morning, with my mother at my side. I remember many things from that night, my mother frantically taking my sister to my aunt's house, sitting in the tiny room waiting for an answer and constantly hearing the sounds of two teenaged boys I barely knew. Nothing was done to me in the hospital, and I returned home all the while still hallucinating and very much unaware. This went on for some time, during which I visited a child psychiatrist who told my parents that the "psychiatric bond had been broken" which to them, as it would to any concerned parent who is not a psychiatrist, meant absolutely nothing.

Eventually I was admitted to Unit 35 of the Royal Alexandra Hospital. I remember few things about my first visit there, but what I do remember is engraved deeply on the surface of my memory. There were two girls there who shared the same first name. Both girls had their reasons for being there of course as I had mine, although they most likely were far more aware of their reason than I. There were times while I was there that I was frightened, such as when Katie G. would have sudden outbursts of anger and be sent to the time-out room, a room with a mattress used to allow angry or misbehaved patients to express their feelings in a closed environment. On another occasion I remember one of the staff, I believe she was a support worker of some kind, saying to me "a little birdie told me that today was your grad" to which I replied "no it's tomorrow". It turns out I was incorrect, but the thing was I was so brainwashed by my hallucinations that I had no clue what day it was anymore, nor why I was in the hospital at all. I was so convinced that everything I was hearing was real, because I had never gone through anything of the sort before and I believed that everything I heard was indeed being said. Just like I had heard on May 31st "I don't know how, I don't know why but she can hear us." Hearing "them", even after I was put on antipsychotic medications Seroquel and Risperdal, no longer only consisted of two teenage boys, but also members of my family and far stranger examples such as my aunt's dog and the Queen of England.

    Hearing that my aunt's dog was performing tricks such as walking around on her hind legs like a human while wearing clothes, and writing everything I did simultaneously seems ridiculously far-fetched as I reflect upon it now. However, because I was so consumed by my ailment I believed it. It's also heartbreaking to think about how I believed that the Queen of England was visiting Edmonton and wished to give me a tiara, which my parents locked in a safe in our home. Yet, despite my seamless lack of insight during this rough time in my life I never told a soul about either of these instances. However, there were countless examples of times where I did tell my parents what I was hearing. One such example was when I was trying to go to bed and I heard that three girls from my school, that I didn't particularly like, at the time, were spray-painting our retaining wall. Another was when I told my dad, while in the car with him, that my aunt had told me that we were related to a Canadian pop singer that shares the same last name as his grandmother's maiden name. Thinking about this almost five years later brings a chill to my bones. The pain these memories contain breaks my heart, but the progress I have made since then is enough to ease my mind, if not in it's entirely than at least in parts. Although after the passing of my hallucinations came another set hurdles.

As if beginning high school isn't enough stress I began high school as another person entirely. Journal entries from August 2006 describe my fear of starting school because of being constantly tired, worrying about getting lost in a new school and facing my peers now that they knew I had been sick. I also described a fear of the bus rides to come as my first boyfriend, who took the same bus, had recently dumped me. In addition I feared the return of the voices that had plagued me for several weeks. Yet I had no clue just how bad things were about to become.

For months I battled demons such as an extra forty pounds that came on in a flash, but took months of nearly starving myself and hours and hours on the treadmill to overcome. I remember my pediatrician making me see him monthly, bullying me as I was forced to weigh in at his office, or at least that's how it felt a t the time. I hated the way I ate so much less and worked out harder than I had ever before, but could not lose an ounce. Even now the faded stretch marks remind me of the torment I dealt with and drive me insane. Yet the weight was only a small part of the battle. I became what my mom describes as a zombie, I lost all my friends at school I barely uttered a word and my grades in school were for the first time in my life mediocre. By October, not only was I at my heaviest, but I was also a complete zombie. My mother was concerned as I was speaking less and less, and my take on this was I did not know what to say. If only I could have shown her then that things would change. Although my first semester of high school was difficult, I slowly began to lose weight, make new friends and rekindle my relationship with old ones too. Saying that those months were easy would be a lie however. Yet some part of me never gave up, and I am thankful to this day that I worked as hard as I did that year.

    April 24th, 2007
During the last seven months I have stopped taking Risperdal. I am slowly becoming more talkative, and closer to my old self as each day goes by. I have noticed a great increase in my scholarly achievements; however I will be taking Math 10 Pure in July. From the events of last May-June I have ultimately gained a vast knowledge about myself and life in general. I'm 95% back to myself. I hope to continue to stay healthy.

    What I know Now (April 2007)
Things can change drastically, very quickly.
You may seem healthy, but that can change.
There aren't really any answers.
    If something dramatic happens in life, people are going to treat you differently.
You have to suffer for what isn't in your control.

There are people who can help.
With time, you can get your life on track.
    There is a lot of wisdom, to what my much younger self once wrote, yet it's quite unsettling for a young girl to have to think so pessimistically about life. If I have learned anything since I was in the tenth grade it has been that I have a tremendous amount of

support around me. Saying that one must suffer for what isn't in one's control is an accurate statement in some respects, because as my life began to go back to normal, it sprung right out of control once again.

No sooner had I stepped outside of my high school doors and began Math 10 in summer school, did everything that had destroyed my summer previous, come right back to bite me. Once again I began to hallucinate, and on July 10th 2007, what used to be a called a schizophrena-form episode, became an ugly diagnosis of schizophrenia. Something I would have nothing of. Most of the summer I was angry in fact, I had never been so angry in my life, and I directed most of it towards my own mother. However, when I received this diagnosis I redirected my anger towards my psychiatrist at the time. I wrote two feisty essays for him and tested his diagnosis. My attitude was that I was not going to be diagnosed with schizophrenia without a fight. The pain I felt throughout that depressive episode was far worse than anything I had ever experienced before. I had random jarring pains that would come and go as they pleased all over my body, for the first month and a half that I spent in my regular high school, ABJ, before hospitalization I couldn't sleep and kept hearing the sound of my ex-boyfriend's voice. It was because I was hearing his voice that made things so much harder, what I heard was he wanted to get back together, and I acted accordingly. I embarrassed myself in many ways because of my hallucinations and confronted him a few times before realizing that I was indeed sick all over again. As time went on, and my newly reborn auditory hallucinations plagued my existence, I began to lose hope in myself all together.

October 13th, 2007

Since the beginning of school I have felt as if I don't belong. I finally attempted to leave this earth last Friday night. My mom is making me feel horrible because I feel as if everything I try to do is wrong, I've been crying everyday and I e-mailed some friends about my depression and my mom won't allow me to make my own choices. I wish I could spend time doing what I want but I feel guilty and my mom is never happy for me. My tears won't end because my life is slowly being forgotten and I still want to die, I'm going to the Royal Alex on Monday again and I want to stay as long as possible because I know how much I'm hated at home and at school. I wish I could have a happy life again but I know nobody really cares when I'm at home, so I envy life outside of it, if my mom truly loves me why do I feel ashamed to be myself? Will I ever be loved again? My mom is always getting mad at me and my dad and I wish there was a way I could make everyone happy but my own life is not worth my mom's time. I hate myself more than ever and I wish someone cared, I do not believe I should live if I am such a burden to the woman, who gave birth to me. I only want to stay in the hospital because I know there will be professionals who won't judge me as being wimpy, stupid or simply unworthy of my own happiness. Zoloft at 150mg would not even help me. Now all I wish I could have is someone who would care about me no matter what.

I felt worthless for quite some time and even though it was not rational I believed that my own mother hated me as much as I hated myself. Evidently my mother was angry with me and I was angry with her for the whole summer and I had begun to believe that there was no way of pleasing her. Yet even after I caused her grief for almost four months, she never left my side as I embarked on my second journey to Unit 35.

The largest difference between my second stay and my previous one was my placement in the Unit. Unlike the last time I was no longer on lockdown, I had a roommate and even I went to school, which for me was filled with crafts and going on the computer checking my e-mail, and Facebook. Motivation was never something I lacked. I wanted to continue my work sent from my high school more than anything. In fact I managed to read a novel for French class, and I completed my biology homework until I could no longer do so.

It was in Unit 35 that we obtained a second opinion on my diagnosis and it was then that I received my vindication. I was given a choice for the first time since I was 15. For the first time since before I became ill there was hope that my previous self could return. ECT was the option and although there has been a lot of controversy regarding the treatment, going through with it meant having an answer. If the hallucinations stopped, I was simply depressed; if they continued after treatment, I was schizophrenic and would be sentenced to a new medication that promised regular blood tests and more weight gain. Nevertheless, just like anything in life there was a lot of waiting involved. It wasn't until November 19th that I received my first treatment and on the day before my first treatment I once again felt helpless.

November 18th, 2007
For the last few weeks I've felt pretty miserable. After the Royal Alex, I felt I had improved, however the last 3 weeks have been very difficult at the Glenrose. My stomach barely agrees with me and my memory is nothing like before. I find I'm agitated much more often and I am continuing to hallucinate. I felt as if I didn't belong when I was at the Glenrose, but I know I'm not even close to being ready for ABJ again. I miss the extra-curricular activities at my old school. I have made a few friends in each hospital and I only wish I could be like my old self. Tomorrow I'm going to receive my first ECT treatment in order to reverse all my symptoms.

My fear of what the future was to hold strangled me. At that point in my life I wanted nothing more than normalcy, yet I knew it was something I would have to wait for. I was prepared for the inevitable shocks to my brain, but not for the aftermath.

November 27th, 2007
Today wasn't the best day for me. I'm finding most of the kids in here to be quite immature. As I sit by the window, I begin to reminisce about the summer before I got sick again. I have no clue why it's taking me so long to recover. I feel sick to my stomach, head

throbbing, and impatient, but by now I'm used to the chaos. Every morning is just another day of screaming and debates. Next, we eat, drink and I listen to the sound of voices, grunts and sounds of stupid things like I'd just entered a class in the middle of a food fight. Ear plugs could never compete with the current group of kids. I don't know how I'll ever forgive myself for the months of agony I suffered for. In emergency, last time (on Monday) I overdosed on Elavil as a suicide attempt, I can only remember needles poking into my hand and now thinking of the coolness of my blood and the danger I put myself in, I pray that I'll never allow myself to do something that stupid again. I know that no matter how sick I may be now, I will never allow my depression to prevent my recovery.

Although the ECT was erasing my hallucinations I was still very unstable at that point in time. Proof of this was my second attempt at overdosing which to my mother's dismay, worked quite well. Remembering a nurse in the emergency room poking me several times with a needle and my mother holding me up still makes me feel sick to my stomach. I was hypothermic, frozen by my own means. It breaks my heart to think of the hell I put my mom through that morning, imagining the fear I caused brings a gut-wrenching feeling of guilt. I cannot imagine how she must have felt seeing her daughter wishing to be dead by her own sword. It was enough to push a person well over the edge, but with a strength that could only come from a higher power she and I persevered. That night my body sought its payback and as became a prisoner to the toilet. This punishment was a breeze however in comparison to what could have happened. I was lucky, I did not suffer organ failure, I did not require CPR or the use of a defibrillator to jump-start a failing heart. All that happened to me was a long sleep, an angry stomach and guilt which began to form the next day.

On November 28th 2007, I described feeling horrible for letting my mom down. I also realized how much I depended on the routine of going to school which included leadership meetings on Wednesdays, lunch hours with friends, and French, my favourite class for as long as I had been in school. The swim team which I had joined was yet another thing I longed for. "I feel as if every time I could have a nice swim I'm stuck feeling annoyed with kids who are 13 acting like four year olds." My level of frustration continued to grow as I finished my ECT treatments and returned to the Glenrose as a day patient, because although there were a few people who I enjoyed spending time with, there were many more who to me were equivalent to a pack of hyenas. School there was a joke for me, at that point I had nothing left to do but wait for February, when I could return to the familiarity of my high school.

As December came and went, my inevitable return to school became an object of fear for my mother, and although I did not show it, I was also afraid. Her fear was result of my zombie-like behaviour, of which I once again could not recognize in myself. As January rolled around, I began taking drivers ed. on Monday and Fridays and continued going to the Glenrose Tuesday through Thursday. While there I did grade nine Math because my teacher figured it would help me because I still had not completed Math 10. It was simple for me, as it had been the first time, which proved nothing for me, as I knew already that it was completely irrelevant knowledge for Math 10. The whole experience proved to be nothing more than a boring distraction once again and I continued to day-dream about returning to my high school. With school only weeks away, my worries about the upcoming semester kicked in. I had a loaded semester ahead which included Math, English, Chemistry, Biology by correspondence, and Social Studies. Although I had a lot on my plate I never ceased to want more, a huge part of me wanted to date again, which never happened, and another part of me wanted a job which in a few months I acquired.

     By April my life was once again back on track, I was doing well in school, I got my drivers license and had just started working at Swiss Chalet. Biology by correspondence was on its way and I had decided to leave Math 10 for the summer. During that semester I also became very aware of how sick I was only months before and when prompted to write a poem for my English class, I wrote of what I knew best.

Where Am I?
One day I woke up alive, yet dead.
Visible on the outside, fine, but broken within.
As I spoke, people failed to see the hidden torment.
At the highest does of antidepressants, I drowned in my tears.
Sorrow controlled me like a dictator.
Few noticed the mutation, and those who did denied it.
Left class in tears, grades sunk deeper than the Titanic.
One day, I hit the floor, willpower to get up vanished.
Where was I? What happened to my smile?

My mouth was as dry as a desert.
The only fluid contained was blood.
Even my tears were running low.
Spirit was damaged; life hated and death envied.
Tried every tonic, but my mood wouldn't improve.
Wasn't in school; couldn't see my friends.
I found a cruet of pills, took about half the bottle and woke up in hell.
By the sound of sick patients and drug addicts, and the look on my mom's face I knew I was in the ER.
The fluorescent lighting blinded me, the stench of the hospital too familiar, and sleep overtook me.
Became hypothermic; nurses couldn't get any blood.
My wish for death had almost come true.
Why did my mom protect me?
Why was I here?
I allowed myself to become consumed by my infirmity.
When I was in agony, I distracted myself by inflicting pain somewhere else.
To see blood was my wish.
Dug a hole in my thumb, tore away at the skin, but nothing would come.
Sprayed perfume on my wound, knowing it would irritate it.
It hurt for all of a second and then it surpassed.
Was a prisoner, forced to follow a five-year-old's schedule.
Drank my juice, took naps, had no choices.

After a few shocks to my brain, learned that there was hope.
I woke up and found myself once again.
Where I had been, I vowed to never rebound.
I may not smile as often as someone next to me.
I may take pills to keep me content, yet I am here, alive.
When I cry, I feel pain, but when it's over...
I know where I am.

After completing my grade eleven year, and finishing Math 10 over the summer, I returned to school in the fall of 2008 knowing that although I had missed about half semester, I was going to graduate on time. It was a year that would finish one chapter of my life and open the next. Although my grades weren't spectacular, I was doing just fine. Yet after my marks from first semester dropped after my Diploma exams, there became evidence of yet another mountain for me to climb. Memory loss, something my mom had picked up on before anyone else and something that went on to plague not only my results from my second semester of grade twelve, but also my first year of post-secondary.

Despite the frustration that came with taking exams, overall my grade twelve year was a fun-filled experience, filled with an embarrassing crush on a guy who ended up being far less great than I had originally believed, new friends, a family trip to Mexico, and even more poetry. It makes me cringe thinking about the guy who at the time I would have loved to have gone out with. He was perhaps the most obnoxious guy in my graduating class but I found him to be hilarious. Yet like many of my crushes over the years he could have cared less who I was and for that reason I became quite poetically inspired.

Clam
Will you remember the name of that shy girl?
The one often forgotten just another clam
without a pearl
When you walk across that stage and give your
class one last glance
Will you regret never giving her a fair chance?
She always noticed when something made you
sigh,
She silently smiled when she saw the twinkle in
your eye.
But you were too good to care
You would see her
And secretly swear

She was no one special and you never failed to conform.
Spending time with her was not your norm
So one day when you passed by
You obviously didn't recognize the girl with tears in her eye
She was just another page in the book of people you've met,
You didn't remember her, and you had no regret
So when you heard the news the next day you had no clue
That the girl who passed away truly cared about you
Of course you would never remember that shy girl,
For who cares about a clam that has no pearl?

    The emotions I felt in regards to that boy were nothing new for me, but indicate a pain that was much deeper than anything being ignored by a guy at school could create. Even though I had a great group of friends a part of me was evidently not satisfied with my life. Once again I was struggling in Math, this time Math 30, and no matter how hard I would study it wouldn't stick. In addition, Chemistry 30 was also proving to be very difficult. In a journal entry in April I described feeling like an idiot according to my despite hours and hours of studying. I was also stressed about making my schedule for University without any help from my mom. "I cried everyday for the past week and on top of that I'm sick so I don't know what to do. She told me I'll have no support next year (from councilors is what she meant) but I'd like to hope that I could have her support at least. She keeps saying that if I don't like it here I should move out and part of me wants to just run away and live in my car except for the fact that I don't own it and I know better than to give up on my goals. I don't know if my mom is hiding her own emotions of having to let me go so soon or if her true feelings are that she doesn't care what I do with my life and would rather have me give up and try working at a restaurant for the rest of my life. "At that point in the year I had just dropped out of Math 30 and couldn't take any more stress, and was simply seeking her advice which she would not give. I turned to school counselors, my aunt, my psychologist, anyone I could get help from and even began writing advice to others through Youth One, an online support network for teens.

    The chaos between my mom and I eventually did subside as it always has, yet when I started to turn to writing rather dark poetry again her concern rose again for my mental health.

Tears
Pain
A daze that ceases to end
Silence...only on the outside
Inside: the complete absence of peace...
Inner torture
Fear, fear, fear...
The unknown, fear of falling... lying in darkness, alone... helpless

Words
Only words yet they mean more to me...
Words kill
Words scar
Scars that fail to heal...
Rip me apart, leave my heart in shreds
Mind feels blank yet is overflowing with feelings
locked up inside
My heart tells me to release my emotions
...better judgment says: do not worry others
Where are the answers?
What is my fate?
Will I die alone in my misery...
Or slowly break down the bolts that have closed me in?
Not a soul has a clue
Not me, nor you

It seems so evident now of what was to come, yet for almost three years I was fine. I finished Math 30 during the summer and in the fall I began my first year of University at Campus St. Jean. During the school year I made new friends, and dealt with the SSDS, Specialized Student Disability Services. I received accommodations for my exams, yet became victim to my poor memory. Because of what can only be described as a fuzzy memory, and study habits, which I later found out to be useless, my GPA fell just short of the standard required, to be accepted into the faculty of Education. After a psychological assessment, which should have been done before I entered post-secondary I rediscovered a sense of hope. I proved to be intelligent as ever, with a fuzzy memory, which was something that would be catered to upon my return to school in the fall. The only thing in my way was something nobody predicted happening; my illness would once again show its darker side, yet this time in a much different way.

Nothing that occurred thus far could have predicted what happened. I worked full-time with a full-spectrum of people, and performed the simple and very boring task of copying and pasting on the computer. My job could be simply described as computer work consisting of Ctrl+V, Ctrl+C, sprinkled with the occasional use of the spacebar and the enter key and topped off with clicking. I was lucky as always to get away from work and venture to Idaho in July, and Disneyland in August. Yet things got to me I guess. My mom and I fought for most of the summer, I was stressed about the upcoming school year, my task at work was about to change, and my boyfriend of a few months was moving to Vancouver. Maybe it was the stress of the transition at work that got to me, I broke down when talking to my supervisor before I left, and although I didn't have to be at work for more than a couple hours and had planned on going golfing, the golf game never happened. It was at that moment that my mind took over. When leaving work instead of turning right, I went left and began my journey north.

I began in Mundare buying a couple magazines some snacks and three lottery tickets. I then proceeded to go north on gravel roads and ran out of gas a few times that night. I knocked on several doors with no answer before I found a young family who lent me there phone, as I left my cell phone at work. I called my mom letting her know where I was and telling her I would be home in about an hour. It was the first of four calls I made that night. Each time she urged me to go home and I told her I would. The first time I ran out of gas a young guy drove me to get a Jerry can of about 15L. I then continued north and ran out of gas a second time, after paying 40$ on a gas pump that gave me nothing. Because I was unaware of the pump not working I continued to drive waiting for the dial on my fuel level to go back up, only to run out half way between two gas stations. I received a 5L Jerry can of gas outside of Smoky Lake which was supposed to be enough to get my vehicle to the nearest station. Yet because I was angry about paying for gas and getting none I turned the other way. Once almost half way I looked at the Range Roads and realized that I was no longer nearly as East from home as I had been. At that point I continued West on my way home. About an hour North of home, on a gravel road I ran out again. At this point, I met a man who's son worked with my dad and he gave me the little bit of gas he had. Once again I called my mom. Knowing that I was nearing home, I began to fear getting in trouble and headed north once again. Because I was driving on primarily gravel roads there were no service stations for miles, running out of fuel again was inevitable. The fourth time I ran out of gas I was no longer on gravel road but was once again way north, outside the County of Athabasca. I walked up a driveway and met an elderly woman. It was approximately 9 o'clock and I called my mom who notified my dad who had barely started his shift at work. He spoke to the woman and then to her son and told me to drive towards Nanton and stay there. I promised my dad I would meet him there, but the man had given me enough fuel to get home and I was determined to that instead. Once I could see the city lights I felt afraid once again.

      Suicidal thoughts took over. I drove down a gravel road, one of many I ventured on that night and mixed a concoction of a smoothie and nail polish and washed down about 3500-5000mg of Ibuprofen and organic Gravol. The nail polish and organic Gravol tasted so disgusting that I spit a lot of the liquid out, in attempt to rid myself of the taste. I then took my broken windshield wiper off my car and tried to cut my ankle which didn't work. Searching through the contents of my vehicle I found wire cutters and cut my ankle. I took a sharpie and crossed out my tattoo of the word 'Believe' and wrote stopped believing on my arm. I then started writing a letter on the pages of the magazines I had bought earlier that day. I threw the letter outside my car and drove a bit more. I wrote about how I would divide the money if I won the lottery, planning to give a portion to my boyfriend and his family, two of my aunts and uncles, and my parents. I did this all in attempt to make a paper trail that would lead my parents and the police in the wrong direction. I threw out my pants, and the coveralls that I had acquired from a guy at work, earlier that day. It was my goal to lead anyone who wanted to find me in the opposite direction. I took out my shoelaces and tied them together and stuck them around my neck and pulled them tighter and tighter. I then drove off the road and into the ditch hitting a tree. I went into the back seat pulled on the shoelaces around my neck tighter and tighter. I then tied the rubber from my broken windshield around my left ankle in attempt to cut off my circulation. Lastly, I prayed for forgiveness and planned to hang myself from a tree.

Yet before I parked, I had begun to listen to Shine FM, a Christian Radio station and while I was hurting myself uplifting music played which made me realize that I was making a huge mistake.

I backed out of the ditch and headed north again towards where I was supposed to meet my dad. Once again, I drifted onto a gravel road, and had to go to the bathroom like crazy. I hopped out of my vehicle while leaving my socks in shoes inside to avoid peeing on them. All I had on was underwear, a bra and a t-shirt. It was no sooner that I stepped outside that I realized I locked my keys inside. Using what I had left in me I sat on the hood of my car trying to keep warm. I was stuck in the middle of nowhere, it was dark and cold. My survival instinct kicked in, I began pulling out tall grass from the ditch a piling it underneath my vehicle. I found a fallen tree on the other side of the road and dragged it over. I continued piling mud, and grass until the entire diver's side of my vehicle was filled from right underneath to the gravel below. It so windy and cold, and once again I feared for my life. I got back onto the hood of my vehicle and prayed for the wind to stop. It seemed to subside for a moment, but picked up once again, so I began screaming for help and running towards acreages. To my luck, dogs heard me and began barking like crazy. I went up the driveway and a kid came out telling the dogs to shut up. I screamed for help and finally an answer. Embarrassed I pulled down my t-shirt and explained I had gotten out of my car to go pee, and locked myself out. They graciously let me in, gave me sweats and made me warm coffee. It was a proof of the goodness in humanity.

    Once clothed, I immediately called home. I then spoke with the police who had been called in Nanton at 11. It was now two in the morning and my parents were both home after my dad had given up looking for me. I remember feeling so afraid of getting in trouble, yet my parents were anything but angry. In fact, I had scared them probably a lot more than I can imagine even now. While at the family's house, I went on Facebook and update my status, for a reason that escapes me. I also wrote an incomprehensible e-mail to my boss, which I rediscovered weeks later. It had something to do with wanting to have my office moved and the possibility of me quitting. My parents arrived with my dad's truck at around 4 am and had to boost my Rav., with cables provided by the family who's house I had arrived at. The drive home was about an hour and a half and the entire time I spoke. Once we got home, my mom told me to shower and to go straight to bed. Yet just like almost every night that week, I could not. I got up and told my parents about my overdose. My mom told me to pack my bags and I did. I hopped in the car as my mouth was running a mile a minute, and I was crying at the same time which must have sounded hilarious because I noticed my mom and dad laugh as I sat in my mom's car and waited. "Another word and you're going to the Alex!" was the last thing my mom said before we left. Because of my absolute fear of the adult psych ward at the Royal Alex due to a murder that occurred there, I managed to stay quiet until we reached the Grey Nuns.

Upon arrival in the empty Emergency Room on Saturday morning I told the nurse about my overdose and how I had tried to use the rubber or the windshield wiper as a tourniquet. Shortly after speaking with the nurse I was moved to a tiny room with my mom where we waited for hours. I remember getting an ECG, and being told that non-invasive cardiologists are needed. Memories of feeling anxious and hearing talking outside the room also come to mind, in fact I believe that once I began hearing things it disturbed my mom and at that moment she left. My last memory of emergency that morning, was when a security guard walked in and said he could tell I was getting was anxious and wondered what they could do to alleviate my stress.

October 1st 2010,
My mother thinks I'm manic, because I woke up at six. The only reason why I did so was because I had to go to the bathroom, and my sister's alarm clock went off after I woke up. My Seroquel just got lowered yesterday to 450mg, and my Lithium increased back to 600mg, because my levels were low. I hate my life right now. There I was minding my own business making a flyer for tutoring for January

as I will have only have seven and a half hours of class a week, attending only Monday, Wednesday, and Friday. As soon as she comes upstairs and sees me doing something other than writing my book she starts a fight. My contract at work is finished December 31st and I will be unemployed once again. I have two years experience tutoring and am an Education student what's the big deal? I even have a two hour break each day to work on assignments and study. Her argument is that maybe second year courses are harder, to which I answered I already took second and third year courses last year and my best mark was in a second year Education course! She argued back that this is my last chance, which I will give her that it's true, if I don't score a GPA of 2.0 or higher I will be on Academic probation, or even worse, kicked out! Yet here's the thing, I took 5 courses a semester last year, I'm taking three in January, and I even specifically chose the easiest courses for myself in order to guarantee success. On top of that I am getting a tutor and a learning strategist through all this to help me with my study skills and help me work around my fuzzy memory. What can go wrong was my take on it, with all that help, and having the option of only taking two courses due to medical concerns I'm wondering what I'll do with all my time. Yet my mom says I'm being irrational, okay well then I'll let her think that. I'm fine, I'm not manic. I had six to seven hours of sleep last night, I wasn't up all night, yet because before I needed between 10 and 12 hours and was still tired I'm manic! The worst of it is tomorrow I'm supposed to be going to a workshop from nine until three, and she just finished telling me I'm not allowed to go. I've been looking forward to it since she mentioned it yesterday morning. It's an introduction to clowning, how much more fun can you add to my day? Yet due to the fact that we had a fight over a flyer I was making, she says I can't go. Does she not realize how badly I want something to do with my life? All my friends, and that is not an exaggeration, every single one of them, is in school! On top of that most of them are in school and working! Me, I'm not working yet, and when I go back, hopefully next week, I'll only be working 16 hours a week split into three days. Meaning I have four days of waking up, eating, working out and sleeping, which some people might envy, but come on... I'm no slacker!

    I love having more energy, for the first time in over a month I'm not half-dead! That should be a good thing should it not? Today the treadmill was easy, in fact I probably could've doubled my time on it if I wanted to. I cleaned the basement, I went through my whole room again and organized things perfectly, I made McKayla's birthday card and worked on her gift, I visited an old friend at the barn... I can go on and on about the things I accomplished today, I feel fantastic. Just because I don't normally feel energetic at six and seven in the morning doesn't mean I can't start right? It's great to be up early, I get so much more done, and the hours of the day feel endless when I wake up. I could easily argue my point for hours, especially right now. Maybe I am a bit manic. Hypo-manic let's say, but still, my Lithium levels are soon going to increase, so what's the issue? My doctor told me if I start having nights where I'm not sleeping to let him know. Well last night was not a night without sleep, it was a night with less sleep than usual, but six to seven hours of sleep is healthy. Yet according to my mom it isn't when I'm on "that much" Seroquel. He dropped it by 150mg what do you expect? On top of that, all the working out I've been most definitely has contributed to my energy levels.

Looking back at that lengthy tangent about "not being manic" it is evident that my mother was right. For context, for many years I only took 50mg of Seroquel and it knocked me out cold!

Today was a day that I needed. My mom woke me up at around 8 and drove my sister to her volleyball tournament and me to the Caring Clowns workshop, which she told me I wasn't going to twice including once in the car. It's ironic that I was at a clown workshop because my mind has been working overtime lately and therefore clowning comes easily. My mother however, who has always had a short fuse is especially short with me, when it's best to just let things slide. Or in this case soar down a slide similar to the Sky Screamer at the West Edmonton Mall World Waterpark. It's always been a battle between me and my mother and the only reason why I'm writing this now, during my younger sister's family birthday party is that for her treat bags we bought 3 inch Vinylmation figurines for each cousin other than Brianna who will be four in December and her brother Ethan, who received t-shirts. My cousin Matthew, who will be eight in January, received the Finding Nemo

Vinylmation which I had my eye on while in Disneyland and I asked him if he would trade for my green dinosaur which he was hesitant about. I proceeded to tell him that it was his choice and he did not have to, but I figured it was more boyish and he may want it more than the bright yellow submarine Nemo. After they left my mom confronted me and told me I should not have done so, which angered me, because my mom has been picking fights with me all day and I have been up since eight on my feet and helping her with this party afterwards and am tired.

To say my mom was picking fights also seems very one-sided, because although we tend to clash at the best of times, I can now, as a fully cognitively developed adult, admit that I am just as responsible for any conflict that occurs with my mother and I. I am also very grateful, to this day, for all the help she has given me over the years and continues to do so.

I am upstairs now, in my room, in peace; where I cannot be bothered by her or anyone else that may have a beef with me. I like the solitude; it makes me feel at ease right now after a day filled with professional clowns, and my own clowns, my family. It's also a good way to be hypo-manic or manic whichever it may be and silent. I can write for hours this way except for the fact that in about an hour I'll be taking my meds which knock me out rather promptly.

I took my meds now because it's essential to me that I be alert and ready to drive in order to go to work. If this works, taking them an hour early, I will be able to drive and return to work, starting later, but functioning. Ah, the inevitable Seroquel haze. I can feel it creeping in already. It's been about 45 minutes, now just wait 'til I try and stand up. Slowly is key, 'cause I'll be up and down and hitting my head on my bed post again all in second or less! I am finally about to call it a night after playing some more with my clown things. It's 10:37 and it's amazing that I'm not passed out on my bedroom floor. Off to bed it shall be 'cause there is no way I can stay up any more.

October 5th, 2010
Now I understand where she's coming from. I feel terrible, I feel typical, I feel wrong. Today was my first day back at work and while cleaning out a file cabinet I found evidence of a problem much bigger than I could have ever guessed. It all makes sense to me now, the missed pizza party, the showing up to work late, the feeling sick and tired over and over again. In this girl's top drawer was Senecot, Colase, Minocyclene. It's sad how we all made assumptions, but I must say she hid it well. She would eat a big meal for breakfast when she got to work, and take those pills, and maybe even throw up. Her energy came from the pops she would drink, sweet and full of caffeine, but according to my other coworker never finished. Probably too many calories. It's quite sad how that works. She would always wear baggy sweatshirts and skinny jeans, and it was perfect. Even people who are overweight can have thin legs, and it was always cold in that trailer this summer, I seldom took off my coat. Her disease was eating away at her,

and like "Dr. Phil" has said time and time again, it's the mental illness with the highest mortality rate. Hopefully someone will be alerted and will approach her as I know how hard it can be to admit needing help, and for her illness it's going to be a tough road to recovery.

    On a much lighter side I got the contact information for clowning at the Scotford Christmas party. Now all I have to do is get a hold of the people in charge and call the clowns to let them know I'm in. Today was a very good day aside from the guilt-trip I gave myself when finding out abut. My coworker's condition. I spoke to Donald for most likely over an hour, Fred for probably close to the same amount of time, and also John. Coming at nine was quite entertaining though because when I called both Fred and John they were at a meeting together and away from the phone. Luckily I met up with a lady in the hallway who gave me John's number so I could call him after Fred did not pick up. While waiting I also met up with a man named Leo who also knows my dad and who gave me Vern's number so he could escort me from the Admin building to the Training trailer, under the scaffolding that covered the door.

    After work however things slowly escalated to the point where I swore and yelled once again at my own mother. I really wanted to go to ABJ to speak with the school chaplain, Mrs. K, who I will always be tempted to call Ms. B as she got married the summer I graduated. On top of that I wanted also to speak to my former French and social studies teacher, the academic counsellor, my grade 11 social teacher and my bio 20 and 30 teacher. Yet once again my mom's answer to that was no, you don't need to go today. My mistake being manic of course meant that I would not take no for an answer, somewhat like a door to door salesperson.

    Anyway, we were at OLPH for McKayla's volleyball game and the team she was playing against was from Vegreville, and was quite loud; like the Holy Spirit team, Heat, was this past weekend. Because I worked today I was already sort of tired because I woke up at 8 and worked until 3, and the game was starting after 4pm. In addition to being tired, it had been already 4 hours since I had eaten last therefore my blood sugar was also low, which most likely; on these meds, probably had a much higher impact that it would normally.

    What I said to my mom was "why can't I go for a walk?"
    To which to she answered "that's not what you said."
    To which I retorted I'm going to be 20 years old, I'm not a f****ng baby. Which made her turn around because that is the one word she could nor stand, and I used it loosely and I do not believe I have ever before. The ride home was silent, but once we got home things escalated once again. My mom and I continued to argue, as it is something I do a lot of when manic and, this time my dad yelled at both of us, which shut both me and my mom up for good.

I have been recently diagnosed with Bi-Polar Disorder after 7 years, plus of heartache after heartache, 3 suicide attempts and at least 9 different medications. On top of that I have had two psychotic episodes, one at 15, the next at 17, and I underwent ECT to treat my associated depression as well. In addition, I have suffered from anxiety and panic attacks my whole life, I remember at 4 years old staying up all night in my bed thinking and not knowing that it was not normal for a 4-year-old to have adult stress levels. When finally treated, I was 12 and began getting so sick that I couldn't hold down food, and I went for help thinking I had a weird eating disorder, with little body image issues, and it turns out I was just anxious. I would recommend ECT to anyone who is afraid as It saved my life two years ago in a way that no med could, It jumpstarted my brain and I felt remarkably better after only 1 treatment. That is how I would explain my struggle to an outsider, or even a member of my family. It's so hard these days to get anywhere with people despite our efforts to communicate things. But a neuro-psychologist I met up with twice gave me the best analogy to explain ECT to me, because it was thought to be the root of my memory issues. Her husband like my grandpa had to have by-pass surgery in his heart and she said just like by-pass surgery reboots the heart, ECT reboots the brain. It should have been obvious to me from the get-go, and in a way it was, but hearing the comparison is really what hit home for me.

More time has passed, and I'm not even allowed to be on the internet at this point which leaves me stranded in ways you cannot even begin to imagine. Yesterday, while on the phone with my boyfriend for not even 15 minutes, after him calling me from Vancouver, my mom told me to get off the phone. My mom and I got into a huge fight and he was only trying to console a suicidal me. All week I've been battling with my mother, who got mad at me on Monday for making plans at the mall for coffee with friends. I didn't even have coffee; I had an iced chai tea latte, basically tea in milk with ice cubes so it wouldn't have too much caffeine. On top of that I bought a book, a young adult's guide to dealing with Bipolar or a title of the sort, but I'm scared to bring it out from hiding in my room, for the fear of getting caught reading something I paid nearly 20$ for. I hate the secrecy of our relationship on my end I feel awful, but the only reason why I'm so secretive is out of fear of further confrontation. She's got me so afraid of doing anything wrong at this point that my nerves are driving me mad. I hate my life as it is right now and what makes it worse is my mom always thinks I'm blaming things on her. She tells me to grow up, and screams at me about the stupidity of Facebook, which honestly there's no harm in what I've done on there. In fact right now I've set the privacy settings to the max, in order to avoid my family and certain acquaintances from work judging me. Her thing is pick up the phone and talk to people, well how can I do that when she won't let me call? She also hates texting, like it's from Satan too and all I can say is, because I have to be in front of her while talking to my boyfriend, and I can't have my laptop in my room, and the phone is too expensive, what else do I have to actually have some privacy in my life?

Privacy is the biggest thing I have lost this year, and this summer made it slowly dwindle to nothing as she found out things she never should have about my relationship with my boyfriend. Some of the behaviour was atypical of me, but still I was battling mania, depression and my parents and working full-time so what the heck did I have to relax about. Nothing! As soon as I tried to go to family member's homes, for some source of comfort, I had to face an angry mother. It didn't matter if it was my dad's parents, or siblings or her parents or sisters, as long as I tried to seek comfort from anyone other than I don't know, maybe God, she would treat me like I was betraying her. Anyways I better eat my dinner before that starts a fight...

Turns out my mom is missing in action, I'm not sure what she's doing, it says Rainbow sale or Rainbow gala on the calendar and McKayla also had volleyball practice I believe. My dad went to work about a half an hour ago and right now I'm basically pondering if I should go on the treadmill now or wait an hour. It really doesn't matter, I don't have any commitments tomorrow morning but I do have a meeting with my teacher at one in the afternoon, and a coffee date with a childhood friend seven. Tomorrow should be a really good day, visiting mature people who aren't related to me is one of my favourite things to do, in fact that old teacher of mine was more of my friend during high school anyways.

Today has been not bad, other than the mom not speaking to me bit, at work I had no rights to edit OTIS and therefore had nothing to do but compare what we have, to what is on the old system and test things out in word and online to make sure everything is working. I also spent time texting friends and foes, and even checked my personal e-mail and Facebook messages during my break. It was a weird scenario today, as the training trailer was nearly empty during most of the day. It didn't really matter to me though because my bosses told me to just relax, do the work I could, although there wasn't much, and take it easy. As my boss always says, don't worry, we are paid by the hour, which in today's case I was almost paid to sit there and look pretty! On my break I also wrote an interesting poem in my notebook, which I brought home to get the songs I heard on the radio and liked, for my iPod and to recopy the poem, or at least rip it out. It was the perfect analogy, comparing myself to a cookie...

Sometimes I feel like the sun will never shine, it's almost officially winter, snow has covered the ground, it's December 4th. Today was the kids party for my dad's workplace. I went as a clown and helped another veteran-clown as I showed off my borrowed magic tricks and he made possibly fifty balloon dogs along with roughly that many swords. It was a side-gig of course, as my true calling as far as clowning will truly reside in the nursing homes and hospitals. It's not an easy job being a clown, unless of course I'm hypo-manic and bursting with energy, because my anxiety and recent constant tiredness drag me down. I am now on four meds: Lithium, Epival (Valproic acid), Seroquel, and Abilify.

Each one with different side-effects and Epival and Abilify being the two new ones are giving me so many different feeling I'm not sure if I still have a cold or if it's my meds that are causing my congestion and cough. In addition, I am now once again, really hungry, getting more acne despite my use of different cleansers and lotions, and tired when I wake up, by 4pm, and once again before 9. To add to this turmoil as if I haven't complained enough already, I'm definitely not going back to school in January, because like my mom and psychologist both say I need to have been stable for a couple months before I even begin to but that sort of stress on the table. It's hard to believe that I am going to end up missing more than just a semester; a time limit that I already felt was too much. A whole year would be absolutely devastating and I can't imagine how I will cope with this new reality, especially now that my contract at work cannot be extended. Clowning as much as possible and going to OLPH to volunteer or even tutoring will be my only sense of release from sitting at home and doing nothing exciting. My mom however and my psychologist on our last visit did help me feel sort of at ease by saying that I could take guitar lessons and pick up a new sport, which I would love to take up tennis or even get back into taekwondo. Perhaps even an aerobics type class or basic triathlon training would help keep me fit and happy. No matter what I do with the time I am about to have, I hope to return at full capacity when I am indeed ready for school.

Sometimes I feel like it would be nice to take a bunch of pictures of myself and pretend to have a proper social life. I know that January is going to make things worse. When one friend took a semester off she was travelling the Asian side world, and I'll be at home trying to get some sort of normalcy back into my life, while attempting to enjoy a situation my health put me in, and I struggled to get out of until now: a point where I know that nothing will change, I am trapped. There is nothing I can do at this point, my dreams of continuing my education and graduating on time if I took a Spring session and worked hard are gone. I know it's University and that means everyone starts and ends at a different time, but this is me we're talking about, not someone who needed to upgrade high school or someone who wanted to travel for a year. I didn't even need to worry about finances when it came to University because I have parents who have saved money for the purpose of my sister and my education. No, I do not want to wait until September, I would love to go back to school as my old self and pretend that my last hospitalization was just a nightmare, or even a tiny setback, but when I get sick, as many other mental health patients do, I turn into a person I do not wish to be. Not only do I go to a slum in my mind that ceases to end, but now I have the added aspect of mania, a much different yet equally frightening for other people to observe, especially my mother who has always been inconveniently for her, on the bad end of my antics. It's quite frightening to imagine all the things that could happen to me in a mixed state of mind, which is the way I have been feeling most often these last three months.

      A solution has finally been found. After months of trying to convince my new doctor that ECT was the way to go I am two treatments in and feeling hopeful. I know that two treatments is not quite a point at which I should feel ready to smile, but I do feel slightly better. I have more energy, something I have been lacking for the longest time due to meds, frustration and depression. All I wanted was a fix that wouldn't take weeks to months and give countless side-effects but my mother and I played tug-a-war with the doctor until two weeks ago. Yet here I am preparing for another nine months without school, jobless, bored, and lonely. My plan to make this time fun and not overwhelming is to learn guitar, after nearly three years of stalling, take up a new sport, perhaps tennis, and if I'm feeling really good, and my mind is working well enough by March or so to take correspondence courses from Université Laval. In addition to all of that, my mom is going to teach me how to cook, which is something I will definitely need to learn, and quickly.

      Three treatments down and anywhere between 5 and 9 left. I don't really feel any different, it's so much harder to tell if it's working because I'm still on four meds. Epival, Litthium, Seroquel, and Abilify: 750

mg for the first two, 150mg of Seroquel and 10mg of Abilify. I am drugged, and I feel it. My mom gets angry and tells me to force myself out of bed, but it's nearly impossible to do so especially when I know that I have nothing to do during the day anyways. I am no longer living and I haven't been living for quite some time. I've gone from having little enthusiasm in life, to nearly none at all. My brain is so tired and feels overworked even though I have hardly anything to stimulate it right now. As I write this tears come to my eyes because I miss being happy, and being in control. Right now the illness has control over me. I am at a low that goes so deep within me that I can barely snap out of it. The hardest part about this low is that I know things aren't going to be the way I want them for another 9 months. It's January 2nd, and I must wait until September to go to school and return to a "normal" life. Having no job, no school, and an illness that ultimately screw up your entire body with or without medications with terrible side-effects is something that I wish on no one. Yet here I am suffering the effects, waiting for my life to return to normal.

      Where is my hope? I guess I lost it while drifting further and further away from where I once was. Thinking of better days should give me hope that there will be similar times in the future, yet the exact opposite is occurring. Right now I feel like those good times are simply memories because my life has been so drastically changed since the end of August and not for the better. I only wish that I could speak to someone about how I feel and not be put down for "complaining". I am not normal by any means right now, even by my own standards. I am a mess, crying at nearly everything, hyper-sensitive, tired all the time, in physical pain while conjuring up these words, and holding back tears. I've been told by far too many people, not only family that I am loved by them, which I whole-heartedly believe but at this point I am too ready to give up. I feel as though I've been hanging onto a rope suspended in the air from a plane, and no matter how strong I may be, gravity is pulling me down. My illness is gravity, and the rope is the love of my family and friends. It turns out that my illness is stronger lately and if I didn't think suicide was a selfish choice that would hurt more people than it would help I'd already be gone. I have enough ideas pertaining to how I would succeed. There are so many chemicals to drink in this household, and there are big knives in the kitchen among other things. I've got enough meds to really damage my internal organs, and in the winter it's not hard to freeze to death, if I was stealth enough to escape. The scariest part of all these thoughts is they don't frighten me anymore, they seem perfectly normal and although I know that my last breaths would be painful, it would be much easier to be dead than it is to live with many of the symptoms of bipolar disorder.

  Fight, fight, fight, fight, fight, fight! A chant that I will never participate in, mostly because of the amount of guilt and pure grief I feel after arguing with my mother. She must enjoy it, because it seems that whenever I even begin to get involved with a boy she is there with her hurtful words prepared to take on someone with twice the amount of emotional strength as I posses. The subject whose name I will not mention happened to be someone who I had never met before, and because of this she decided that there were far too many reasons not to get involved. My faults in the matter were I claimed he was in my psychology class last year, but it turns out we met via Facebook, a fact I did not reveal to her until today. I still cannot stop crying however because although I may not want to jump into a relationship with this guy, it does not mean that everything my mom has to say about me is true. I am not a desperate, easily manipulated little girl like she believes; all I want is respect and this guy gave it to me last night, not attempting to take advantage of me like my mom automatically assumes. She now screams that I'm going manic again, which all I can say to that is that is complete nonsense and I am fine! I'd rather kill myself ten times over than put up with this crap. My mom wants me out and quite frankly I want out too, but there's no place for me to go.

    I am so upset right now that I could use a whole box of tissues and still not be finished crying. The boy from last night, that helped trigger this whole fight has offered me a roof over my head to live with him rent free, but the thing is I know that would be wrong, even if there was a way of getting to his place from here and moving some things, I would feel uncomfortable moving in with someone I barely know at all, it wouldn't be rational, at this point. I would miss my dog, the treadmill, having a vehicle, a comfy bed, and all my stuff. No matter how bad things get here, I know I have to try and listen to my mom, no matter how wrong I think she is, and how sick to my stomach our fights make me feel.

All this chaos in our home today is really making me wonder about ECT. Now that I've had four treatments I wonder how things are supposed to be at this point if different at all. My meds are all the same except for the Seroquel which my doctor wants me to be off of all together. I am now on only 75mg of it, as of last night, but it's hard for me to tell if there is a difference between one day and the next when it comes to a med change. Right now I feel worse than I have in about a month, but that's always the case when my mom and I fight. I feel worthless, stupid, unloved and anything else she may actually tell me, like today, being useless and weak the former her actually saying and the latter being my interpretation of what being easily swayed or manipulated truly means. I thought I was supposed to feel less depressed but tomorrow, when I fill in the pre-ECT survey I will be answering with how I feel at this very moment in mind.

It's Friday, another day of treatment and another day in the life of a manic-depressive. Right now I am home with my dog, and my dad who happens to be sleeping off of a night shift. My sister is in school, obviously and my mom is at her school to volunteer for the hot lunch program. I am bored, sitting downstairs typing away because I can't get internet on my laptop, most likely because of my mom's wish to keep me away from all boys until I am healthy. Even this thought brings tears to my eyes, as I know what it's like to wish for a normal life again and to not get it. I mean I want someone there for me who isn't just a friend, I'm not desperate, but when there are guys interested, why not see what can happen?

      I know why not: because my mom won't have it. She has never liked a single person I have dated or wished to date, other than maybe my first boyfriend who I dated when I was 14 and 15, but not until after my psychologist and I persuaded her into letting me date him. I think my mom sees me as a child when I'm sick, someone who can't take care of herself in any regard. Yesterday she even told my dad I was manic! Like that's the case, if I was manic I wouldn't be here, I'd be driving somewhere far away to get away from all of this. I'd stay in a hotel, or just sleep in my car for an hour or so and keep going. I'd bring my passport, cross the border and hope that nobody would find me, or I'd drive east on the Yellowhead, and hope to eventually hit Québec.
Yet I'm not manic, and although those ideas occur in my head, I know exactly what would happen and where I would be if I went through with them.

      The thought of hospitalization is something that makes my stomach uneasy. I cannot stand it, I felt powerless, bored, lazy and hungry when I was there the latter being because of my lack of taste for any of the meals. In fact once I moved onto the open unit I began to eat less and less because I hated the food. Right now, I wish I could say the same about our meals at home, or any food we have in our house. My hunger is a monster far bigger than I am, and lately I've been struggling to not give in. I think of food constantly and even my mom has noticed that I am eating a bit more than I was before. Not enough to cause me to gain weight, but if I don't get in line soon that'll be the next burden upon me.

Thank goodness I have things to distract me from food, such as clowning, friends and now a potential boyfriend with whom I had coffee with and am going skating with followed by dinner this coming Saturday. ECT must be helping me because I have finally come to terms with the fact that being out of school until September does not have to be the end of me. Volunteering is something I would really like to do more of because it always makes me feel good inside, and with Edmonton Caring Clowns I get to experience laughter and love in a way that no other form of volunteer service could provide. It's like an anti-depressant that actually works. Laughter therapy is not only rewarding for the senior's I am visiting but also very much so, for me. In fact, I'm not sure who benefits more from it, me or them! It's actually sort of crazy to think back five months; while I was hospitalized I was a much different person than I am currently...

My fist few days were rough, nothing I wrote made any sense and although I was being drugged with what my mom called "enough to sedate a horse", I was still waking up several times a night to the sounds of another patient who ended up scaring me senseless and making me desperate to get out of the locked unit as quickly as possible.

On August 28th at 4:29 am I wrote this: "Very sedate had sleeping and antidepressant sucked now this."

"Thank the angel looking for me that night I was very resourceful."

On September 1st, at 4 am, this: "Sorry on a side note I'm eating and water coffee twice awck my grandmas did it at 70 hasn't smocked yet until a skill hill they, b they would bero keep quiet cause it can be loud."

I managed to translate and retract what a wrote in a way that doesn't entirely match up to what was sort of written on those early mornings making the mixed up text read like this...

August 28th
"Very sedated, antidepressants being weaned. It's terrible but I believe that an angel came to visit. On a side note, I'm sorry because I put everyone through this trouble."

September 1st
"I HATE BEING ALONE, but as long as Nadine keeps contradicting me I will stay here."

I was very lucky in those early days in the hospital to have so many visitors, especially my boyfriend at the time, in fact there are many anecdotes in my writings from the hospital that mention me speaking to him and feeling relieved and thankful for his kindness and understanding during my sickest days.

"2 mg Ativan Argument 10:30 pm"
"Nadine will not be quiet, she bangs on her door constantly and is furious as she got her meds today, for the first time in a while after throwing them out without being caught before. Being a nurse practitioner may mean she's smart but it does not mean she's an easy patient to handle. She frightens me, and makes me want to never leave my room when she is out of hers. I hope everything will begin to work out in my favour soon, so I can move away from this place to a quieter and safer unit."

Once again at this point I felt very thankful for the love of my boyfriend at the time that went over and above his expected duty and continued not to judge me although it must have been very hard.
What lead to my third hospitalization was possibly the most fearful moments of my parents' lives. The way in which I described it in my hospital writing is most likely not the most accurate way of describing that night therefore I have chosen to describe it both from what I have recorded in writing and what my memory recalls.

August 30th,
"First off to clarify, the police were invited, (a way of wording I would only use if manic) but not in the way of arresting me. I ran away from home and attempted suicide, nearly managing to succeed. It gave me faith to hold on. I prayed for 5 hours (probably only an hour) and asked for forgiveness for a long time for what I had done and what I was about to do. I slept for almost three hours in a field (a fact

which looking back I believe to be completely false, I may have slept only for approximately 20 minutes if I did sleep at all. I was however, in a field but in my vehicle) I was 300km from home (or close to it) and made a noose and tightened it, preparing to hang myself in the wee hours of the morning."

There are so many blank spaces in my writing from the hospital that it is very easy to tell just how scattered my mind was at the beginning of it all. To complete the story of how I managed to get in the hospital I must recount everything from the beginning...

"It was my last day of work for the week and I had finished my responsibilities for the day... as usual early! I'm not sure what triggered me that day but instead of heading home from work I turned the opposite direction. I began driving through small towns and went first to Andrew and picked up some groceries and lottery tickets. I then travelled on many gravel raids, through many small towns all the while calling my mom at home and each time promising to come home. When it got darker I began to think thoughts that looking back made no sense I started writing letters and throwing things out of the vehicle making a "trail" to be found. During all this I ran out of gas at least three times and had such luck with people helping me fill up with small Jerry cans. One stroke of bad luck however that occurred was in Smoky Lake when I thought I was filling up and I paid over 40$ for no fuel. My parents were of course worried sick and my dad even came off of a night shift to try and find me after I called home then got a hold of my dad at an elderly woman's home outside of Athabasca County. The final leg of my journey was spent with me driving past where I was supposed to meet my dad, seeing city lights, turning around then running out of gas all over again. At this point I has thrown out my pants somewhere along the way and had to go to the bathroom like crazy. I then proceeded to exit my vehicle leaving my socks and shoes inside of it locking myself out. At this point it was freezing outside, pitch black and windy. My survival instincts then kicked in. I began pulling out the long grass and grabbing mud and fallen trees pilling it under my vehicle to make a shelter. I also sat on the hood of the Rav to keep warm, but as time went on and the sweat I had built up while making the shelter under my vehicle disappeared and the engine cooled off I knew I had to do something else. I started by praying for the wind to die down, which for a minute of two it seemed to do just that, yet knowing that my whereabouts was unknown to my parents I decided that I should jog up the gravel road and hope to find a nice safe home. Thinking about our own dog and her hearing capabilities I decided to scream as loud as I could the word HELP! Soon dogs heard me along with a nice family and they let me in to their home, provided me with warm clothes, hot coffee and what I needed most since my cell phone was at work, a phone! I immediately called my parents, it was around two in the morning and I was supposed to be home before five pm the day before. The police were then contacted once again and the search was off. At around 4 my parents arrived, boosted my vehicle and we headed home. I rode home with my dad and managed to talk the whole way back. Upon arriving home I took a shower and then was told to go to bed, but couldn't sleep. It was then that it became obvious that I was manic and needed to be hospitalized. The final words I remember her saying as we left our home were... "You say one more word and I'm taking you to the Alex!", and with a threat like that there was no way that I was going to speak again."

    I chose to retell this part of the story because it was such a crucial part to me transitioning into the adult psychiatric system. It demonstrated just how immature I was at nineteen and how much growth and self-discovery would occur in the years to come.

    June 28th, 2021
    "It was a long week and in the wee hours of Friday morning I was restless. I decided at two that I would get up and be productive, do some prep for my group and make myself far more prepared for my upcoming shift. I had celebrated my grad with my boyfriend as he drove up to visit me, and it was a great night. I bought myself an expensive bottle of champagne and we sipped it and shared it. It was a great night including a lot of intimacy, flirting me ranting about work and us continuing to get to know one another. We had only been dating for not quite two months at this point and we had begun talking almost a month before we had our first date. I lived in High Prairie still at that point and visited him both in Grande Prairie in early May and in the Fawcett Lake Area in camp three times while working and taking random days off, not only to see him, but to help me

prepare for my move and due to having to take sick time to recover from my tonsillectomy.

I am now quite tired, but my mind is still quite restless due to having him in my space. It's nothing against him but I am so used to being alone and I can't handle this kind of thing just yet. This is something I don't wish to tell him, because in time it'll change, but I need to do something else and I don't want to hurt him or sabotage something that is only beginning due to my own anxiety.

This lone wolf sort of complex I had developed really lingered a lot further into our relationship than I intended, but like all things in life things improved within my own mind and as I finish the final edits on this "masterpiece" I can say I have never been happier in a romantic relationship and we have now been living together for nearly five full months, which will be even longer by the time this book is in someone else's hands!

This is mostly the end of the narrative, but I wanted to write a little bit about my most recent stint in the hospital. I could feel my mental health challenges rising shortly after I moved to the city. Environmental noises of sirens and the bus stop keeping me awake, trauma I haven't dealt with that I'm going to address in therapy in the new year with a brand-new therapist. A new job, new expectations, and not knowing what tools were being used on site, bigger units, a hospital way larger than where I have ever worked, specialized programs, community resources I needed to learn myself before I could refer people to them. All this work stress, and then co-habituating for the first time, getting used to someone else's way of cooking and cleaning, sort of falling into a domesticated role and having to adjust to this. Cooking and cleaning after two people is way harder than one. Add a second dog to the mix and the vacuuming never ends. Sharing laundry and a yard with the tenants downstairs, a city garbage collection system that is way less convenient than going to the transfer station for free. All these changes and my ability to cope did not align. My anxiety was unbearable, every morning I would wake up and dry heave as I made my coffee, occasionally at night I would full-on vomit. It was so difficult for me to manage, because then manic symptoms came next, hallucinations, everything felt out of my control, until I begged to be taken to the Grey Nuns Hospital again. My boyfriend took me, then my sister took over the night shift until I got a bed. This bed I slept on, or tried to in the chaos of emergency, Saturday and Sunday nights and eventually at around 3:30pm I got a bed in psych, and shared a room with two other women, just over a week and started ECT once more. I received a few treatments, while in hospital then more as a outpatient. It helped, just as it had in the past with my depression, the psychosis, and the mania. I am on a higher dose of two meds I have been on for years, and on a medication for my anxiety that is allowing me to function, without all the extra worry, dry heaving, and other physical and mental symptoms plaguing me all day long. I am off work for a bit, it has already been a couple weeks and I hope to go back in a couple weeks, depending on what my doctor says next week. I'm stubborn when it comes to work, but work gives me a purpose, and an income, which right now is very uncertain because I applied for medical Employment Insurance, and it is still under review. I know this won't pay much eve n if I do get it, but it's better than the alternative which is no paycheque at all, due to being casual. Even today I did a job interview for three positions, and although I was nervous, I feel like it went a lot of better than my previous interview where I knew I really bombed. The rest of this tale now will be bits of poetry here and there that I have compiled over the years, it's far more playful for the most part, than the narrative you have likely just completed reading (or skimming at least!) Of note these are not in any chronological order and were simply added as they were found in various journals, notes on my phone, etc.

Dreamer Dreamer

Was she bad
No, just Dreamer
The shy one

Nah that was a ploy in a parking lot

This one has lots to say

What a terrorist

Only the cutest kind of course

Yes she's a handful

But she definitely keeps me on my toes and keeps me warm at night and she sleeps on my legs or under my bed

She's a cutie for sure

She knows how to use her good looks to get her way too

Puppy dog eyes for days that one

Dreaming of being a good dog or something…

How Many Is Too Many Oreos

Serving sizes or suggestions

Half a cup of ice cream

No way in hell are you restricting my dessert calories

Everything else sure, but if I'm not eating this meal everyday, then don't bother

Dessert, a treat, a cheat nope

Whoever invented the concept of a cheat day really didn't have a lot going on the rest of the week, so let's prescribe binge eating instead

No thank you

Diet culture is not for me and guess what

I maintained weight loss better not counting calories anyway

So there, I burst that bubble just like gum

Pop, pop, pop… flavours gone

Neck Pain
Swtiching meds
And the state of a coma
My brain is dying inside
Help me please I'm on knees
You are the best medicine
Matt…
Consider this my first love poem and it has been officially dedicated to you
I hope to remain yours for as long as you will let me
For when we first met in person, you asked me if I would let you do many things.
And most of those things we haven't quite yet done.
Yet you have done for me so much more than what I could have ever dreamed.
You are the one I adore.
I love you, dear.
Let me become your "My Maria"

My heart may be a country song, but you make me feel my best punk rock self, for it has always been who I truly am.

She was a beautiful mess, to put it lightly
Nothing about her was light however
Every emotion she felt was so heavy it weighed on her like a coffin just waiting to be filled with her pathetic corpse
She felt guilty for crimes she didn't commit and snide comments she didn't dare escape her lips
Punishing herself was her coping mechanism, a tonic that poisoned her soul
Her tears could drown a fish
Her heart was broken and glued back together, but nonetheless it shattered daily like glass
Many people tried to help her pick up the pieces over the years, but each time it was mended less and less was preserved
One day she hoped things would be different, she wouldn't be so fragile, so impressionable

One day maybe she'd stand up for herself once and for all prove to herself more than anyone else that she was strong
One day perhaps, but for now she is still so weak

Document 19...
In a row, wow that's a milestone, journals beware

That's all there is to say about that

Rat-a-tat-tat

Yes I can scat, like a cat...

Open that door, or climb on the floor

Rhyming is easy is you want I can show you

But why would we go there, it is only to show flow

What scheme is that

Well it's no limerick, nor a haiku

Oooh, ooh ooh were you thinking it too?

Yes it's not too challenging, think syllables not words and it'll be great
You can even skate

What is your pay rate

Probably not enough to enough to pay for gas

But do not fret you can earn some extra cash, cutting grass

There is a lot to say
Or maybe not but I ain't cray cray

Or if I am my doctor doesn't it know it yet

And by the time he does, let's just say we forget

Rhymes, all the time

Fine it won't rhyme but why not, for I do love lime

Is it over yet

Or has the threshold not been met

Just don't get wet!

Things You Need To Know Before Dating the Terribly Anxious

Well, I used to put up a Red Flag list, but then I learned that I was not the issue

In fact, being told you're "hard to love" might be even more abusive than "no one will ever love you like I do"

Guess what, I didn't want to be "loved" in that way anyway...

Put downs, emotional abuse, gas lighting and silent treatment are not my problem.

"I didn't even cheat on you" Is not a compliment to me, it's almost like you're trying to stroke your own ego again.

"Don't let your head swell"

Wow so when my self image isn't in the garbage it's not right, but you can tell me for an entire hour while you are drunk the whole time that all the women in the bar are watching you, no they are probably watching me pay the bill again and drive your drunk ass home.

It took me six years to say that! SIX YEARS!

For those in the back or those in that booth, stand up for yourselves or find someone who will and run like the hills.

You are worthy of love, and not the lack of it for what you are not lacking!

Plague Doctor Fifel
What is your question this morning?
Why should I answer?
Who do I follow for the information?
For are no leader.

I am losing respect
You're attitude is like a plague
Covid-19
You are the virus
Go back to Mexico and drink more Coronas

Good bye

Dear me, forget
Forget you are no longer in his power, his plague is fictitious
Ignore him tonight and in your subconscious

Good evening
Maria
This is your sister, here is a friend, here is Icky

We are your soldiers

We are your posse
We are your team
And together we lead one another to success

In time this will improve for you are strong

Plague doctors were unqualified til recently anyway.

I love one horse towns, long dirt roads and watching the Northern Lights
I love apples, cinnamon and pumpkin pie
I live for far out dreams pastures and movies with random themes
I love pug smiles, bird laughs and Halloween
The sound of the whistling prairie wind
The smell of, of… gasoline
Dressing up nice in my old blue jeans
I live for sunrises, sunsets and words kept in, but not forgotten
I live for memories like faded pictures sitting in an old shoe box
I love the feeling of a crisp autumn day
The sound of a chickadee
But who would have thought a poem without you would be simply about me

There's a Long Time to Go Unless You Feel Like Leaving Now

Funny how when we are young all we want to be is grown up, and once we get there and start paying bills we wish we would have stayed children a little longer

Life seems to fly by faster the older you get

But it may seem like we're aging backwards if we have someone in our life lapping on life stages

Sometimes it's a matter of perspective

So now where's these poems I was talking about eh?

Is this book merely rants…

Nah but sometimes rants are poems, you don't have to follow a rhyme scheme to get it right.

Where's the rhymes? Do we do it all the time?

I'm no Dr. Seuss, you picked up the wrong book, the cover must have caught your eye

Pugs will do that, you know

Right when you least expect it they'll pull you in

We all want to live in a fairy land dream world

Cotton candy skies and lakes of lemonade

Not quite reality, but sometimes it's nice to dream

It would seem

It would really tickle your medulla oblongata

Sometimes we need a translation on brainstem eh?

Really Canadian, "just out for a rip?"

Nah I wanted to grab a Mickey and some darts, to take one drag and vomit.

The Covid 2021

There couldn't be a book released in a pandemic that doesn't address it right
When does a pandemic become an endemic
Well it my opinion it never truly ends
It's like anything in life really
Your first crush in high school
That birthmark on your abdomen
All the things we wish you could get rid of but truly can't

Covid-Scmovid am I right?

I have nothing but horrible things to say about the healthcare system handling that, but I don't want to rant.

I am burned out beyond belief, I'm just grateful I'm not a nurse.

All is well in Covid land, yet only because I have managed to not get it in the two years that it has nearly been around.

Yup I am triple vaxxed, and ready to face the next mutation or variant as you will.

Oh but my rights and freedoms, right?

I never felt that a vaccine that could help me prevent others from getting sick would be taking anything away from me.

No I'm not so self absorbed that it was something that crossed my mind.

Sorry if you disagree, but I saw people die.

Oh… you didn't, well consider yourself blessed.

No one in my family luckily, but everyone in my family who got Covid was not so lucky to go without symptoms or long Covid.

So tell me again why the massive Canadian flag in the back of your pickup or your F**K the prime minister window sticker is relevant.

There were generations that died for our freedoms, so you want to avoid a near painless prick in your tricep to avoid what, exactly?

End of story, mic drop…
The Secret September 2nd 2021 (warning mushy content overload)

When we started talking there was still snow on the ground.

I lived in Big Lakes County and I followed you to worksites in my spare time.

Our first date was bubble tea and a first kiss in your car in a park I don't even know the name of.

We went on adventures, hiked Berg Lake trail.

Drinking Ginger Beer and being drunk on infatuation more than alcohol.

After our first date I couldn't stop gushing about you.

I told both my sister and a married friend that I had never been so optimistic about a relationship in my life.

My mom approved of you instantly.

My grandpa told me that he already thought I found a husband.

This was August 8th, the evening I intended on going home because you basically kicked me out.

I came back and drove to work, was nearly late for a client.

Since we met I have accomplished so many things.

I'd like to think that meeting you was a big one this year as well.

Sunday August 29th was the day you gave me a cold.

Four months in and even though I question your feelings for me daily, a part of me knows you care about me in a similar fashion as me.

I can't believe how much I've written about my midnight snack. *(Pretty cheesy nickname if you ask me, and somehow that fish named after you is still alive, living off neglect! This little tidbit was added while editing in November of 2022.)*

The one I hope truly is the love of my life.

Words fall out of my pen, but I will keep these thoughts inside because I'm so scared of losing you and we've only survived a season's worth.

First conversations in early April and continuing a long distance relationship five months later.

It's crazy how time flies, I am ready to give myself away emotionally, but the last time I admitted I loved you, it made me feel defeated, childish and afraid.

I long to hear three words so much that I am losing my mind waiting for the feelings or the words reciprocated.

I love you Matthew, and this is why this chapter isn't just written for you, but also directly to you as well.

It's crazy to think that I had to be both drunk, exhausted and sick to write this.

It's almost as if I'm spilling my soul on to these pages from drunken sauteed garlic, an orange bell pepper, Sriracha and an egg.

Ginger beer, vodka, limes.

The recipe to mushy Maria, mushy Wow loves Midnight Snack.

So much that I will probably say it before the wedding, but if I take til then, it's all okay, because it's weeks away. *(The wedding I was referring to being my younger sister's which ironically is when Matthew first told me he loved me, and of course I cried!)*

And now for the sad parts…

I remember that you said a few killer comments that are forever engrained in my mind.

I said one time that I don't need a man to buy me jewelry and you told me not to worry because you wouldn't. *(Something that changed in time, I might add!)*

Another thing that has stuck with me probably since May or June is that your ex wanted to marry you, but you didn't want to marry her. *(I have a far better understanding of that whole situation now!)*

Interestingly enough, I always wanted to get married until I realized I just wasn't wife material.

Many years ago my ex who would have made the most abusive husband I could have asked for browsed for engagement rings.

Now years later I still carry fears of men in general and dating someone who probably could also benefit from therapy, as I have…

It takes a lot out of me emotionally to do my job, and when I feel the need to psycho-analyze you, it's like I'm dating a client. *(Looking at this now I really understand where I was coming from here, but believe it was harsh to word things like that, as much as it's harder for me to get a read on Matthew's emotions, we communicate quite well, and it's something I am really grateful for in our relationship now that we are over a year and a half in and almost five months into me living with him.)*

It's a challenge for sure, but if I had to compare you to climbing a mountain, it would be mount Mulanji, a mountain in Malawi and I would climb that mountain in flip flops that broke in a long skirt, every day for the rest of my life if I could.

My hand may be tired, but the night is young and I long to continue writing…

What this looks like at 1:30 am drunk, exhausted and sipping cold coffee is interesting.

All I want to do is be next to you, but you're asleep and work tomorrow, and I should be resting, not making plans to kiss you before you head to work.

I should be sober, asleep and in my own home.

Yet, here I am alone with Icky in my parent's basement with more lights on than my mom would approve of. *(I find this to be a funny addition to this short paragraph because anyone who enters my parents house at night would notice the lack of lights on, but I am literally the same way now!)*

To be in love once more is a frightening feeling. I long to spend time with you all the time. The gap went from roughly 400km to about 200km, in the words of my colleague, we are "half distance."

Half distance geographically, but maybe double the distance emotionally.

If I didn't want this to work so badly, I would have ended things a month ago if I were to be truly honest...

It hurts for me to write that, but my exes in the past (the only two long term relationships comparisons I have...) both of those boys (men would be an overstatement).

Both confessed feelings for me long before the four-month mark. To not hear that "I love you" is a challenge for me, go someone who has had to be incredibly self-aware.

Sometimes I wonder if you are closed off from all your own trauma, or if you legit are apathetic in your feelings for me.

I have invested months and thousands of words on this relationship. Love letters, gifts, so many kilometers on the Rav, chasing you all over Alberta like a hopelessly addicted soul.

I want nothing more than to know you feel the same way, but as far as I can tell, by the way you act and talk...

You seem indifferent.

You appear to want me physically, but so do pervy patients in psych.

I want a stronger emotional bond with you and unfortunately that requires me to take off my girlfriend hat and put on my Rec.T hat and do some counseling, which is my area of expertise these days apparently. (This pen is literally amazing!!!)

I can thank my former work wife for that without a doubt!

I'm so excited about how non-smudgy it is, I'm distracted from my intrusive thoughts about how you must not care as much as you let on.

I love you… 15 and a half pages of this journal later, it is finally written.

If this makes it to the final manuscript I will sign your copy of the book first. For you may not be the inspiration for publishing, but had we not gone on a ghost tour, we would not have met the woman who told me about self-publishing.

And in the knick of time, "Simple Dude" started playing on my phone and I have been listening to this playlist since roughly 3pm yesterday afternoon.

Maybe it's a sign…

Maybe you have been waiting for me, more than I could even begin to realize, and maybe that's all the evidence I need at 1:55 am on September 2nd, 2021.

New day, new coffee, good sleep.

I still have a cough, and a bit more mucus in my lungs. I'll likely call 811 and get a Covid test today. I'm going to see if I can get a rapid test done, because I have pending plans tomorrow and Sunday I don't want to cancel, but will if I'm sick.

If I were to write down every thought I've had about you today, it would take months, because you haven't left my mind all day.

Some day soon those words will slip and I truly hope they are on the edge of your lips.

"Wake Me Up When September Ends" by Green Day is playing on the Shell Bluetooth speaker and I'm happy to say that when September ends I hope you will still want me the way I want you right now.

Sometimes I must silence the alerts of your texts on my phone, because I'm too hurt to talk. Hopefully one day soon that pattern will end. I've been crazy about you since the day we met, and I simply hope we're on the same page, because a part of me loves you more each day, even though the other part is equally scared away.

Even my puggy wants you around because Icky never had a father figure even though one stuck for 2.5 years and tried to linger even longer. Sometimes I think our shitty exes led us to one another. Yet I'm so scared to lose you, I don't even have the capacity to let you know.

I just want to know that at the end of the day, you love me too.

Writing that made me numb, dizzy and sad…

Maybe it's the pain in my elbow.. maybe it's the lack of food in my system.

Regardless, I wish I wasn't sick…
I want simply to be laying next to you.
If only you wanted me there too.

September 8th, 2021

I had a horrible day overall and talking the ear of the man of my dreams proved to be more helpful than usual.

I looked on the calendar on my phone, July 12th I ambushed him in Edmonton when his gift arrived. *(It was a keychain of an old Kodak film reel with real pictures of us and our adventures that said I love you on the bottom.)*

The 13th, I texted him I loved him and used expletives.

His reaction was lackluster and scared me so much.

Today there was a lot of buildup to it once more.

My work phone went off at around 9 and I answered a client, then texted him I loved him (in the third person).

I turned that phone off, then continued the conversation on my regular cell.

Baby steps… one day hopefully in the not too distant future he will say it back.

I'm impatient somewhat because I haven't dated someone who's taken nearly 5 months from a first date and over five since talking to say it.

My last ex said it first.

We said it so early on. So, for me knowing how I feel and mustering up the courage again nearly two months later for an "aww" breaks my damn heart, it really does.

He treats me so well.

Yet maybe he's leading me on.
It's challenging for me to have to feel like I'm guessing and we've been bickering a bit lately too.

Five months is a long time to invest in someone…
Especially when it feels like it's unrequited love…

I truly hope it isn't…

I've poured out my heart so much.
Letter after letter, mailing them with no response.

No signature on the card attached to my grad gift from June. He has expressed that all the fun dates we go on are how he shows his feelings.

I appreciate them so much, but as much as people say... actions speak louder than words...
To me: words like I love you speak louder than dates.

It's nearly midnight though, my hand is cramping up, I'm tired and need to work tomorrow. I have yet to take my meds. It's because I didn't get home til about 6:30. Today was a long miserable day at work Yet at the end of all the chaos, the first person I wanted to talk to was Matt, even though I was initially quite reluctant.

I love that guy, I truly do, and I'm going to do my very best to be the best I can be so we can continue to have a healthy and hopefully long-lasting relationship.

To go back to my original format of to Matt, for Matt is better in my eyes as you are the one this chapter concerns and you are the one I am hopelessly in love with.

Matt, you are one of the reasons I didn't give into my suicidal thoughts in July and August. I had them again yesterday after too much wedding talk, and too much time dwelling on things at home.

I'm grateful for you so much. I hope one day soon we can be together, but unfortunately know that this weekend you are busy and I simply don't have the energy or the capacity to drive down to see you.

I'm just excited that next week you are supposed to be up here, in Bonnyville.

Thirty five minutes from my house according to the map. Most likely less based on my daring habits.

Goodnight September 8th I guess. It's officially Icky's 4th birthday which is a sign for me to go to sleep!

The Tale Never Told

This will bring you deep down the staircase, watch your head as you go down
There may be spiders, but do not fear there are no skeletons down here
There is a lot of glamour in the darkness, but only the dark may you find
If you are searching for diamonds you will only find dust, but if you look far enough you may just find the key to your deepest desires if you are aware enough to know what they truly are

What are we all looking for anyway
Wealth
The secret to eternal life
Love
Fame or fortune
Or simply to know what truly belongs in our minds

There is nothing far from freedom from the largest sorrows should we give ourselves the opportunity to look within the darkness rather than fear it
There is so little to be found when you are looking
But as they say, stop searching and you will find

The Tale of a Dog Named Icky

My little puggy running through my mind
He may have been gone now for some time, but I can remember it as if it was yesterday we were running around High Prairie, you can do the whole town in a half hour if you want

Not quite like the big city, he didn't want to live here

His life was short, but only the good die young, right?

What a silly little pug, a barking at the tv running around my parents' basement

He was a fast one

No one ever saw pug jogging until they met Dr. Icarus Pug, Ph.D

Icarus what a unique name for a very special pug

No he wasn't a Doug

Not lazy, not famous, but greater than most

The runt of the litter that just didn't quite make it

He will always live in my heart and on my left calf

He was truly a dog without a story that didn't end in peanut butter cupcakes, but beet red velvet instead

Four years of love, snuggles, and snoring on my shoulder

He was the keeper of my heart
My first born pug

He may be the last, but he will always be the best

Rest in Peace and keep barking at the TV, you've got grandma and grandpa up there to annoy and grandma never forgot you either!

The Will to Dream

Sometimes we get lost
Lost in space
Out of sight, even when we look at ourselves in the mirror through our own eyes
Where have you been
In the woods or drowning in a lake
Burned into embers or waiting to be born again
There's always something going on, but never enough to spark a flame
Stillness, the quiet peaceful sound of nothing deafening still as one waits
What are we waiting for?
It is happening before our eyes
Right before us
What are we missing out on
There must be a sign
We are only lost in the darkness for a short time

To Die a Happy Lie

There's an awful lot of fear when it comes to death and dying
One would think that this is the part of life that we dread the most
But what if you have felt more dead inside than living, from far beyond the time you should have barely lived at all.
There are challenges some face that other couldn't even imagine.
There are trials and tribulations that would kill anyone too weak.
There are times when we tread a narrow line between life and death and somehow survive.
We will not ever truly know what it feels like to die until we feel nothing at all.

Yet what afterlife are we given, must we stand trial at the pearly gates.
Are we damned for our sins to hell.
Are we stuck in a place neither here, nor there but in between.
Many who have had near death experiences have claimed they have seen a light or even God.
But do we really know where we are going.
What is heaven like?
Do they let us in regardless?
What about all those sins we committed?
What if we have killed?
What if we have hurt so many people in our lives that we have no one else but ourselves.

Surely not everyone can go to such a magical place.

To die a happy lie, would be to go somewhere far better than this life.
This is why, we need to live as if our days are numbered, for they truly are for everyone.

Don't regret tomorrow what you could have accomplished today.
Seize the day, carpe diem, whatever those nuts all say.
Sometimes
Yes sometimes
IT IS NOT THAT SIMPLE…

Yet we must strive to surpass out expectations of ourselves and strive to be the best we can be.

There is truly no harm in trying.
What we haven't tried will only bring us down, if it is worth succeeding.

To die a happy life, now that is entirely different.
To live life without some form of regret can be damn near impossible, but if we give into guilt we will once again fail to live entirely.

No one is perfect, and although not everyone has committed crimes or broken hearts or even treaded a path of pure evil, there is enough evil in this world to share with everyone around us as it is.

Live until your last breath, because if you don't you will simply live a happy lie, and not truly ever know life.

Take me to the moon and show me the meaning of love…

I'm so happy you are here
Take a seat
OR stand at the counter like you're me, eating just about any meal because your kitchen table is covered…
Or because sitting alone at a table in your own house still scares you.

There's a lot be said when it comes to living alone in the middle of nowhere.
Some people told me I should have a gun.

Well that chapter of five and a half years is behind me.
Yes I am truly happy to say I've moved on.

Cohabitating eh?

Pretty soon there will be more to be said about that I'm sure…
Living in sin.
It's all good, this has been a learning curve in the last week.

Yet it's quite nice to not wake up alone.

It's nice to not miss the one I love after only eight hours.

Yes, it's a challenge to give up the solitude, yet there's a comfort in knowing you are living with someone who loves you like no other has.

Yes it truly is a gift.

Love like any other emotion is hard to describe, if this was a book on love it'd probably be about 7000 pages with several more books on the way.

Yet who wants to read that, the Bible is shorter.

Love to anyone who hasn't experienced it is probably a lot harder than it looks.

Things aren't all fairy tales, sunshine and rainbows that's for sure.

Yet to find someone you couldn't live without and actually know it… well now that's something far too rare in life these days.

There are so many words to say…
If only I could get paid to write them instead.

Very exciting to let them live in a world that is so dark, let's shed some light on happiness

Or simply turn on the lights, maybe light a candle or an oil lamp instead

Or maybe we'll stay in the dark because it brings more spook and excitement as it is!

Can't wait to let you discover the complicated mind that has is mine, but yours to take a dip in the deep end for a moment too!

Write to Your Heart's Content

Perfect, let's go

Let's get this party started

I brought tea and knitting needles

The curse words and arguments one gets around mini chocolate bars and BINGO or a stitch and bitch with little old ladies will make you laugh for ten minutes straight

Now to write, or type

Need that typewriter yesterday

Oh well, that's technology from the past for an old soul tying to not become a hoarder, with the hoarder gene

Let's save that for another day

Like next year perhaps

No rants too long, no tale too short

The freedom of words unwritten, spoken perhaps or only a glimmer in the eye of the socially anxious

Thank you for respecting the "I can't say it because I'm too shy, but will probably spill the beans in the next hour or day anyway".

Let It Shine

Let the light shine, let it shine let that darkness in your soul shine…

Spooky spook

Let it creep and crawl all over the floor, up the walls and down the drain

Creepy crawly little spiders, worms, rats, but not in Alberta or so they say.
Do they need a passport to come from Saskatchewan, or is it New York!

Shine like the moon in a clear sky

Shine like the stars in the country, lying on your back trying to not get eaten alive like mosquitoes

Let it shine or maybe just keep it to yourself

Yeah I'm looking at you, the one that never shuts up!

Run on sentence, motor mouth, can't get a word in edge-wise.

Let it smolder instead…

Sometimes we don't even realize what we could have lost of sabotaged and we not been so afraid and just let life happen.

I must say I didn't see house girlfriend in the cards for June of 2022, but I am certainly so happy to be here.

I think I really misjudged what was truly happening last summer and can honestly say that things have never looked so great for me.

There are so many more things I could say in this book, honestly this thing could compare to lengthy novels in size, but the purpose was not to ramble on as I often do in conversation.

Writers are going to write… and Dreamers are going to destroy things and drink your coffee too!

I am truly a different person than the one who moved up north to High Prairie back in the winter of 2016. I have come so far and those years finding myself, honestly were some of the best years of my life.

I graduated, I found a therapist job in Edmonton, I lost my pug, my kitten and most recently my grandma, but I lived the life I needed to, to flourish and become who I was meant to be.

An independent free spirit who doesn't mind settling down one day either.

Lone wolf or not, I have to admit, being domesticated is fine. I truly love everything about living in the city in my own way. Sure the cows make better friends, but my family is here and I have been given full time hours in a job I thought was going to be a huge risk.

Onwards and upwards soon I know it!

Dreamer is loving being the neighborhood watch and even though she and I are besties for the next couple weeks as our boyfriend (*notice I didn't write "my"*) is working away, we will definitely have our little adventures to the p-a-r-k. soon enough!

Yes life has been hard on me at times, but the only thing I truly needed to know when I was caught in the flames was that I could overcome it all.

I really could, I am grateful that I never truly met death's door because I know now that I wouldn't have been able to help those who I work with every day if I would have truly given up entirely.

Life has given me ups and downs, dead ends and everything in between, but I have only come out stronger each time.

More stubborn, and more motivated to make waves.

The "indomitable spirit of a warrior" was something someone once told me on my Facebook wall, signing books was another comment.

These people believed in me when I didn't even think I could go on.

I can truly say that the support I have around me has merely shifted over the years, but I still have so many people who would miss me if I was gone, and for this it is likely I will never try to overdose or similar ever again. I have too much to do here on earth and I think losing so many people around me is what made me also learn that life is too short to not live everyday as if it were your last. Tomorrow isn't guaranteed, and if we spend too much time worrying about the future, we will lose all that we have to live for today.

Live in the moment and take time to enjoy the little things in life, because we will never truly know the answer to everything, but life is full of lessons and we can all find our way through it with a bit of faith and the help of others, if we are only available to accept it, and if we are not, they will always find a way to help us, even if we don't always see it right away.

Thanks again for reading this far, without readers, writers would starve. I'm lucky to have a day job that pays well or I'd be another starving artist that's for sure.

One day I will hopefully get this book on someone else's shelf, but for now I am simply so happy to have completed what is over a decade worth of work.

Well, to say it was a short journey would be an understatement, from starting this back in 2012, to a several year hiatus I never would have imagined to get this far.

Even reading the final moments of this book complied from last year it's amazing how much can change.

I am so grateful for kindle and self-publishing this is truly a gift.

I have had two books printed in the past, but this is truly my greatest work. The other two were gifts with little cartoon characters and nothing like this.

This was supposed to be oh so much more, but I decided that it was never really a story that would end.

This is not a novel, this is my life.

I am not complete, I can only be so lucky to live a long healthy life, or I could get hit by a bus crossing the street tomorrow.

Life can pass us by so quickly before we know it we're 90 and finding it hard to believe.

Thank you for everyone who read this book, skimmed it, looked at the cover, opted not to read but thought it was cool.

I have dedicated a long time to this project and am truly blessed to have the means to tell my tale.

It is a story of a young woman who became more than expected, even by herself.

To say I'm not proud of where I am today would be an outright lie and I am truly grateful for my parents and my sister for being there through some of the darkest times in my life, I really owe you all my life.

For anyone who has known me in the last two years you know I am very passionate about a lot of things including my career, and to have had the opportunity to learn from so many people over the years has truly made me a far more well-rounded person, not only when I have been in care, but also has a healthcare provider myself.

There are and will always be gaps in our mental health care system, but it has and will always be my goal to create an environment of love and respect inside and outside of the hospital doors.

Thank you once again for getting this far, or for even reading the last few pages here and there. I would be nothing without my readers, all two of you!

In all seriousness I hope that this life brings you nothing but joy and the chance to chase rainbows, Northern Lights and sunsets, just as much as I do.

Page 100 even is where it all began to start to make sense.

July 25th 2024, adding to create edition number two on my three year CTRS Anniversary.

Wow what a summer it has been, visiting Jasper, a town that just burned down this week in early July looking forward to having it be a stop to visit in the fall once more, before the snow flies.

It's been so smoky in the city that yesterday, past the can of "Brava" beer (no copyright infringement!!!) on 153rd Ave on my way to work I saw a magpie and felt like I was driving to hell.

It has been hell on my lungs, I took ventolin three or four times yesterday and once today.

I am attempting to make peace with this and peace with these feelings, dwelling up inside of me. I am trying so hard not to resent my "roomate with benefits" and be a better domesticated partner.

He just brought me ibuprofen while I type in the living room and convinced me to try his lime pop I had gotten him this evening.

It was delicious and this made me feel so much more loved than thirty minutes ago.

I will call him eventually and maybe one day he will be my husband, but for now, let's just say "marriage is outdated."

That is a quote from a male coworker who is married. I'm pretty sure he loves his wife…

So this edition is slightly better, simply because the page numbers are actually accurate.

The hardcover copy should be available in the next few days!

Thanks for the read and I appreciate all the friends and family who have supported me in this venture thus far.

Maria E. Miller

@ickyspaws on Instagram

Made in the USA
Columbia, SC
06 April 2025

065d5259-68c0-4b94-a867-1acb4331072bR01